MAD LIBS®
SHARK ATTACK
MAD LIBS

by Mickie
Matheis

Mad Libs
An Imprint of Penguin Random House

MAD LIBS
Penguin Young Readers Group
An Imprint of Penguin Random House LLC

Concept created by Roger Price & Leonard Stern

Cover illustration by Scott Brooks

Published by Mad Libs,
an imprint of Penguin Random House LLC,
345 Hudson Street, New York, New York 10014.
Printed in the USA.

ISBN 9781524788193
11 10

MAD LIBS

INSTRUCTIONS

MAD LIBS® is a game for people who don't like games! It can be played by one, two, three, four, or forty.

● RIDICULOUSLY SIMPLE DIRECTIONS

In this tablet you will find stories containing blank spaces where words are left out. One player, the READER, selects one of these stories. The READER does not tell anyone what the story is about. Instead, he/she asks the other players, the WRITERS, to give him/her words. These words are used to fill in the blank spaces in the story.

● TO PLAY

The READER asks each WRITER in turn to call out a word—an adjective or a noun or whatever the space calls for—and uses them to fill in the blank spaces in the story. The result is a MAD LIBS® game.

When the READER then reads the completed MAD LIBS® game to the other players, they will discover that they have written a story that is fantastic, screamingly funny, shocking, silly, crazy, or just plain dumb—depending upon which words each WRITER called out.

● EXAMPLE (*Before* and *After*)

" _____ !" he said _____
    EXCLAMATION   ADVERB

as he jumped into his convertible _____ and
                         NOUN

drove off with his _____ wife.
          ADJECTIVE

" **OUCH** !" he said **STUPIDLY**
    EXCLAMATION   ADVERB

as he jumped into his convertible **CAT** and
                         NOUN

drove off with his **BRAVE** wife.
          ADJECTIVE

In case you have forgotten what adjectives, adverbs, nouns, and verbs are, here is a quick review:

An ADJECTIVE describes something or somebody. *Lumpy, soft, ugly, messy,* and *short* are adjectives.

An ADVERB tells how something is done. It modifies a verb and usually ends in "ly." *Modestly, stupidly, greedily,* and *carefully* are adverbs.

A NOUN is the name of a person, place, or thing. *Sidewalk, umbrella, bridle, bathtub,* and *nose* are nouns.

A VERB is an action word. *Run, pitch, jump,* and *swim* are verbs. Put the verbs in past tense if the directions say PAST TENSE. *Ran, pitched, jumped,* and *swam* are verbs in the past tense.

When we ask for A PLACE, we mean any sort of place: a country or city (*Spain, Cleveland*) or a room (*bathroom, kitchen*).

An EXCLAMATION or SILLY WORD is any sort of funny sound, gasp, grunt, or outcry, like *Wow!, Ouch!, Whomp!, Ick!,* and *Gadzooks!*

When we ask for specific words, like a NUMBER, a COLOR, an ANIMAL, or a PART OF THE BODY, we mean a word that is one of those things, like *seven, blue, horse,* or *head.*

When we ask for a PLURAL, it means more than one. For example, *cat* pluralized is *cats.*

MAD LIBS® is fun to play with friends, but you can also play it by yourself! To begin with, DO NOT look at the story on the page below. Fill in the blanks on this page with the words called for. Then, using the words you have selected, fill in the blank spaces in the story.

Now you've created your own hilarious MAD LIBS® game!

PREHISTORIC BEGINNINGS

PLURAL NOUN _____

TYPE OF LIQUID _____

A PLACE _____

NUMBER _____

ADJECTIVE _____

NOUN _____

VERB _____

PLURAL NOUN _____

ADJECTIVE _____

ADJECTIVE _____

NOUN _____

PART OF THE BODY (PLURAL) _____

ANIMAL (PLURAL) _____

CELEBRITY _____

PLURAL NOUN _____

NOUN _____

NUMBER _____

PLURAL NOUN _____

MAD LIBS

SHARK SPECIES, PART 1

Oceans and other bodies of _____ around the world are
<u>TYPE OF LIQUID</u>
populated with sharks, including these fascinating _____:
<u>PLURAL NOUN</u>

- **Hammerhead Shark:** This weird-looking _____
  <u>NOUN</u>

  is best known for its long, narrow _____, which
  <u>PART OF THE BODY</u>

  it uses like a metal detector to sense food, such as stingrays

  _____ along the ocean floor.
  <u>VERB ENDING IN "ING"</u>

- **Tiger Shark:** This shark gets its name from the vertical stripes

  and dark black _____-spots on its body that resemble
  <u>NOUN</u>

  those of a/an _____. This shark is a lean, mean
  <u>ANIMAL</u>

  _____ machine, with a mouthful of sharp
  <u>VERB ENDING IN "ING"</u>

  _____ shaped like a circular saw.
  <u>PLURAL NOUN</u>

- **Bull Shark:** This stocky shark has a/an _____
  <u>ADVERB</u>

  aggressive personality, roughly bumping _____
  <u>ANIMAL (PLURAL)</u>

  and other underwater prey with its _____ to make
  <u>PART OF THE BODY</u>

  sure they are edible. _____, that would hurt!
  <u>EXCLAMATION</u>

MAD LIBS® is fun to play with friends, but you can also play it by yourself! To begin with, DO NOT look at the story on the page below. Fill in the blanks on this page with the words called for. Then, using the words you have selected, fill in the blank spaces in the story.

Now you've created your own hilarious MAD LIBS® game!

GREAT WHITES: A TALE ABOUT TEETH

NOUN _____

ADJECTIVE _____

ADJECTIVE _____

PLURAL NOUN _____

NOUN _____

NUMBER _____

PART OF THE BODY _____

VERB ENDING IN "ING" _____

ADJECTIVE _____

TYPE OF FOOD (PLURAL) _____

COLOR _____

ADVERB _____

VERB ENDING IN "ING" _____

MAD LIBS
GREAT WHITES:
A TALE ABOUT TEETH

_____ scientists learn a lot about sharks by studying their
NOUN

_____ teeth. For example, they can determine if the shark
ADJECTIVE

was large, small, or _____ and what type of sea-
ADJECTIVE

_____ it ate. Did you know that sharks regularly lose their
PLURAL NOUN

teeth? Luckily, a new _____ automatically replaces the lost
NOUN

tooth. Some sharks can lose anywhere from _____ to thirty
NUMBER

thousand teeth in their lifetimes! A shark's teeth are arranged in rows

inside its massive _____, with the front row doing most of
PART OF THE BODY

the _____ as the shark hunts. Teeth have different
VERB ENDING IN "ING"

shapes and uses, depending on the species. For example, sharks that

eat fish have long, _____, needlelike teeth ideal for gripping
ADJECTIVE

slippery _____. Those that feed on crustaceans have
TYPE OF FOOD (PLURAL)

thick teeth that resemble dinner plates. Others, such as the great

_____ shark, have _____ jagged teeth that cut like
COLOR   ADVERB

knives. Taking a look at a shark's teeth is super cool, as long as you're

_____ from a distance!
VERB ENDING IN "ING"

MAD LIBS® is fun to play with friends, but you can also play it by yourself! To begin with, DO NOT look at the story on the page below. Fill in the blanks on this page with the words called for. Then, using the words you have selected, fill in the blank spaces in the story.

Now you've created your own hilarious MAD LIBS® game!

MYTHS AND MISCONCEPTIONS

PLURAL NOUN _____

NOUN _____

VERB ENDING IN "ING" _____

TYPE OF FOOD (PLURAL) _____

PART OF THE BODY _____

ADJECTIVE _____

SILLY WORD _____

TYPE OF LIQUID _____

NOUN _____

ANIMAL _____

ADJECTIVE _____

NUMBER _____

PART OF THE BODY _____

ADJECTIVE _____

PLURAL NOUN _____

MAD⊙LIBS®
MYTHS AND
MISCONCEPTIONS

The biggest myth about sharks is that they purposely attack

human _____, which is why they have been called
          PLURAL NOUN

"_____-eaters." But it's far more likely that sharks simply
        NOUN

mistake people _____ in the ocean for turtles or other
               VERB ENDING IN "ING"

things they like to eat, such as _____. They will take
                                  TYPE OF FOOD (PLURAL)

a test bite with their _____ because they don't have hands
                        PART OF THE BODY

to touch with. When sharks realize humans don't taste particularly

_____, they probably think, "_____, yuck!"
    ADJECTIVE   SILLY WORD

before swimming away. In reality, people have a better chance of getting

injured by a flying cork from a bottle of _____, a/an
                                           TYPE OF LIQUID

_____ falling on their head from a coconut tree, or a/an
    NOUN

_____ stinging them. It's also not true that every shark is
    ANIMAL

enormously _____. For example, the dwarf lantern shark is
            ADJECTIVE

just _____ inches in length—roughly the size of a human
      NUMBER

_____. Sharks have gotten a/an _____
  PART OF THE BODY   ADJECTIVE

reputation over the years, but they actually deserve respect and

_____.
  PLURAL NOUN

MAD LIBS® is fun to play with friends, but you can also play it by yourself! To begin with, DO NOT look at the story on the page below. Fill in the blanks on this page with the words called for. Then, using the words you have selected, fill in the blank spaces in the story.

Now you've created your own hilarious MAD LIBS® game!

IF SHARKS COULD FLY

PLURAL NOUN _____

VERB ENDING IN "ING" _____

NOUN _____

ADJECTIVE _____

NOUN _____

ADVERB _____

PART OF THE BODY _____

NUMBER _____

ADJECTIVE _____

TYPE OF LIQUID _____

PART OF THE BODY _____

ADJECTIVE _____

NUMBER _____

NOUN _____

ANIMAL _____

CELEBRITY _____

MAD LIBS

IF SHARKS COULD FLY

For those adventurous _____ who film sharks
                           PLURAL NOUN

_____ in the wild, capturing a great white
VERB ENDING IN "ING"

_____ breaching on camera is not only unforgettable, it's
NOUN

downright _____. Breaching is when a shark launches itself
         ADJECTIVE

out of the ocean as it's hunting a seal or other fast _____.
                                            NOUN

Watching a breaching shark in slow motion is _____ epic!
                                  ADVERB

The shark leaps, _____-first, anywhere from eight to
               PART OF THE BODY

_____ feet in the air, twists around like a/an _____
NUMBER   ADJECTIVE

acrobat with its prey in its jaws, then drops into the _____ on
                                            TYPE OF LIQUID

its _____, making a/an _____ splash that
    PART OF THE BODY   ADJECTIVE

can often be heard for miles. While it's hard to imagine a/an

_____-pound _____ propelling itself almost
NUMBER   NOUN

entirely out of the ocean with the speed and force of a winged

_____, the great white shark does just that. It's one more
ANIMAL

reason this species of shark is the _____ of the shark world!
                                    CELEBRITY

From SHARK ATTACK! MAD LIBS® • Copyright © 2018 by Penguin Random House LLC.

MAD LIBS® is fun to play with friends, but you can also play it by yourself! To begin with, DO NOT look at the story on the page below. Fill in the blanks on this page with the words called for. Then, using the words you have selected, fill in the blank spaces in the story.

Now you've created your own hilarious MAD LIBS® game!

SHARKS OR DOGS?

ADJECTIVE _____

PLURAL NOUN _____

VERB _____

CELEBRITY _____

SAME CELEBRITY _____

VERB ENDING IN "ING" _____

PART OF THE BODY _____

ADVERB _____

NOUN _____

TYPE OF FOOD _____

TYPE OF LIQUID _____

EXCLAMATION _____

VERB _____

PART OF THE BODY _____

PLURAL NOUN _____

ADJECTIVE _____

MAD LIBS®

SHARKS OR DOGS?

Good news! Your family is getting a/an _____ new pet!

ADJECTIVE

What should it be: a dog or a shark? Both of these _____

PLURAL NOUN

have their good points. For example, dogs are fun to _____

VERB

with. You just have to yell, "Here, _____! Here,

CELEBRITY

_____!" and they will come _____. They'll

SAME CELEBRITY   VERB ENDING IN "ING"

knock you flat on your _____ and _____ lick

PART OF THE BODY   ADVERB

you all over. That's why dogs are called "man's best _____."

NOUN

On the other hand, playing fetch with sharks is awesome. Just take

a/an _____-covered fish, throw it as far as you can out into

TYPE OF FOOD

the _____, and—_____!—watch that shark

TYPE OF LIQUID   EXCLAMATION

_____! Dogs will love you with all their _____, but

VERB   PART OF THE BODY

sharks will protect you from menacing _____. Yes, a dog

PLURAL NOUN

would definitely make a great pet. On the other hand, imagine how

fantastic it would be to tell your teacher that your shark ate your

_____ homework!

ADJECTIVE

MAD LIBS® is fun to play with friends, but you can also play it by yourself! To begin with, DO NOT look at the story on the page below. Fill in the blanks on this page with the words called for. Then, using the words you have selected, fill in the blank spaces in the story.

Now you've created your own hilarious MAD LIBS® game!

WHAT'S ON THE MENU?

NOUN _____

A PLACE _____

VERB _____

NUMBER _____

ADJECTIVE _____

CELEBRITY _____

NOUN _____

TYPE OF LIQUID _____

PLURAL NOUN _____

ADVERB _____

TYPE OF FOOD (PLURAL) _____

COLOR _____

NOUN _____

A PLACE _____

TYPE OF FOOD (PLURAL) _____

PART OF THE BODY _____

ADJECTIVE _____

ADJECTIVE _____

Welcome to the Shark Fin Grill, the best _____-food
                                              NOUN
restaurant in all of (the) _____! Sit back and _____
                            A PLACE   VERB
in our _____-square-foot dining room and enjoy
           NUMBER
_____ dishes prepared by our world-class chef,
      ADJECTIVE
_____. I would suggest starting with our soup of the day,
      CELEBRITY
_____ bisque, a steaming _____ broth with
      NOUN   TYPE OF LIQUID
flavorful chunks of _____, served with our signature
                        PLURAL NOUN
sea-sar salad, a/an _____ hearty helping of crisp greens
                        ADVERB
topped with vine-ripened _____. For your main
                              TYPE OF FOOD (PLURAL)
course, our special tonight is grilled _____-fish, freshly
                                            COLOR
caught from the pristine waters of the _____ Ocean off the
                                            NOUN
coast of (the) _____. Lightly seasoned with minced
                  A PLACE
_____, this dish will absolutely melt in your
      TYPE OF FOOD (PLURAL)
_____. Stop into the Shark Fin Grill soon for
      PART OF THE BODY
a/an _____ bite. You'll be _____ you did!
        ADJECTIVE   ADJECTIVE

MAD LIBS® is fun to play with friends, but you can also play it by yourself! To begin with, DO NOT look at the story on the page below. Fill in the blanks on this page with the words called for. Then, using the words you have selected, fill in the blank spaces in the story.

Now you've created your own hilarious MAD LIBS® game!

GREATEST SHARK MOVIES OF ALL TIME

PLURAL NOUN _____

ADJECTIVE _____

PERSON IN ROOM _____

VERB ENDING IN "ING" _____

PERSON IN ROOM (MALE) _____

SAME PERSON IN ROOM (MALE) _____

COLOR _____

CELEBRITY (MALE) _____

A PLACE _____

NOUN _____

ADJECTIVE _____

PERSON IN ROOM _____

CELEBRITY _____

ADJECTIVE _____

PLURAL NOUN _____

MAD LIBS®
GREATEST SHARK MOVIES
OF ALL TIME

Grab a bucket of hot buttered _____ and check out these
PLURAL NOUN

classic shark movies:

- **Kung Fu Shark**: This animated movie tells the story of a/an

  _____ shark named _____ skilled in the
  ADJECTIVE   PERSON IN ROOM

  ancient art of kung fu _____.
                          VERB ENDING IN "ING"

- **Finding** _____: This is the sweet story of
              PERSON IN ROOM (MALE)

  _____, a little _____ shark
  SAME PERSON IN ROOM (MALE)   COLOR

  whose father, _____, travels to the ends of (the)
                CELEBRITY (MALE)

  _____ to find his son when he goes missing.
  A PLACE

- **Great White and the Seven Sharks**: A monstrous great

  white _____ roams the ocean with his seven
        NOUN

  _____ sidekicks—Bubbles, Coral, Spike, Finn,
  ADJECTIVE

  Crush, _____, and _____.
         PERSON IN ROOM   CELEBRITY

- **Sea Wars**: A/An _____ group of aquatic rebels band
                     ADJECTIVE

  together to fight Shark Nader and his dark forces, restoring

  peace and _____ to the ocean.
            PLURAL NOUN

MAD LIBS® is fun to play with friends, but you can also play it by yourself! To begin with, DO NOT look at the story on the page below. Fill in the blanks on this page with the words called for. Then, using the words you have selected, fill in the blank spaces in the story.

Now you've created your own hilarious MAD LIBS® game!

AN UP CLOSE UNDERWATER ENCOUNTER

PART OF THE BODY _____

ADJECTIVE _____

PLURAL NOUN _____

VERB ENDING IN "ING" _____

ANIMAL _____

PLURAL NOUN _____

TYPE OF LIQUID _____

VERB _____

TYPE OF FOOD (PLURAL) _____

NUMBER _____

NOUN _____

PART OF THE BODY _____

COLOR _____

NOUN _____

ADJECTIVE _____

ANIMAL (PLURAL) _____

CELEBRITY _____

PERSON IN ROOM _____

MAD LIBS
AN UP CLOSE UNDERWATER ENCOUNTER

Swimming with sharks is not for the faint of _____!
PART OF THE BODY

However, cage dives are safe, fun, and _____. It's thrilling to
ADJECTIVE

see great white _____ _____ right in
PLURAL NOUN   VERB ENDING IN "ING"

front of you! Here's how the process works. You'll sail out to

_____-infested waters and put on a wet suit. Then you'll
ANIMAL

climb into a cage made from galvanized steel _____, and
PLURAL NOUN

the crew will slowly lower it into the _____. The cage is
TYPE OF LIQUID

securely tied to the boat, so if at any time you wish to _____
VERB

or exit, you can. Next, the crew will lure sharks over using chum,

which is a mixture of fish and _____. While it may be
TYPE OF FOOD (PLURAL)

terrifying to have a shark not more than _____ inches from
NUMBER

your _____, don't worry, its _____ is too large
NOUN   PART OF THE BODY

to fit through the cage bars. You may also see dolphins, _____
COLOR

_____ turtles, and maybe even _____ humpback
NOUN   ADJECTIVE

_____. Our satisfied cage-diving clients have included
ANIMAL (PLURAL)

_____ and _____. Won't you be next?
CELEBRITY   PERSON IN ROOM

MAD LIBS® is fun to play with friends, but you can also play it by yourself! To begin with, DO NOT look at the story on the page below. Fill in the blanks on this page with the words called for. Then, using the words you have selected, fill in the blank spaces in the story.

Now you've created your own hilarious MAD LIBS® game!

SHARK PARTY

NOUN _____

NUMBER _____

PLURAL NOUN _____

ADJECTIVE _____

VERB ENDING IN "ING" _____

ANIMAL (PLURAL) _____

ADJECTIVE _____

NOUN _____

ADVERB _____

PART OF THE BODY _____

VERB _____

NOUN _____

PLURAL NOUN _____

TYPE OF LIQUID _____

ANIMAL _____

VERB _____

The shark-themed party that my mom and _____ threw

NOUN

when I turned _____ years old was amazing. Ten of my

NUMBER

closest _____ and I spent the day doing _____

PLURAL NOUN   ADJECTIVE

shark stuff. We played a game in our _____ pool called

VERB ENDING IN "ING"

shark toss. The object was to throw little plastic _____

ANIMAL (PLURAL)

through the center of a floaty. Whoever got the most in was the

_____ winner. And, of course, we played pin the fin on the

ADJECTIVE

_____. The decorations were _____ awesome,

NOUN   ADVERB

too. My parents made this cool cardboard cutout of a shark's mouth

that you could stick your _____ in for a photo.

PART OF THE BODY

There were signs all over our lawn that said things such as

Caution: _____ *at Your Own Risk . . .* and *Beware!*

VERB

_____*-Infested Waters . . .* and *Do Not Feed the*

NOUN

_____. There were fin-shaped ice sculptures floating in the

PLURAL NOUN

punch bowl to keep the _____ chilled. There were gifts, too.

TYPE OF LIQUID

My favorite was a giant inflatable pool _____. Since I can't

ANIMAL

_____ with real sharks, this was the next best thing!

VERB

MAD LIBS® is fun to play with friends, but you can also play it by yourself! To begin with, DO NOT look at the story on the page below. Fill in the blanks on this page with the words called for. Then, using the words you have selected, fill in the blank spaces in the story.

Now you've created your own hilarious MAD LIBS® game!

SHARK SPECIES, PART 2

PLURAL NOUN _____

ANIMAL _____

NOUN _____

TYPE OF FOOD (PLURAL) _____

ADJECTIVE _____

PART OF THE BODY _____

VERB _____

TYPE OF LIQUID _____

ADJECTIVE _____

VERB ENDING IN "ING" _____

PART OF THE BODY (PLURAL) _____

ADJECTIVE _____

PLURAL NOUN _____

PLURAL NOUN _____

NOUN _____

Some of the more commonly known species of _____ include:
PLURAL NOUN

- **Whale Shark:** Although this gentle giant is the largest species of aquatic _____, it feeds on the tiniest
ANIMAL
_____ creatures, such as plankton and microscopic
NOUN
_____. It gets its name because of how
TYPE OF FOOD (PLURAL)
massively _____ it is. Each whale shark has unique
ADJECTIVE
spots, like the fingerprints on a human _____.
PART OF THE BODY

- **Mako Shark:** This shark can _____ as fast as a
VERB
cheetah can run. It shoots through the _____ like
TYPE OF LIQUID
a/an _____ torpedo. When it's provoked, the mako
ADJECTIVE
will start _____ in a figure eight pattern, lunging
VERB ENDING IN "ING"
at its target with its daggerlike _____ bared.
PART OF THE BODY (PLURAL)

- **Great White Shark:** This _____ predator hunts
ADJECTIVE
with speed, force, and deadly _____. Its mouth
PLURAL NOUN
contains three hundred large, triangular _____. The
PLURAL NOUN
only creature capable of taking on a great white is the killer
_____!
NOUN

MAD LIBS® is fun to play with friends, but you can also play it by yourself! To begin with, DO NOT look at the story on the page below. Fill in the blanks on this page with the words called for. Then, using the words you have selected, fill in the blank spaces in the story.

Now you've created your own hilarious MAD LIBS® game!

ODE TO THE GREAT WHITE

NOUN _____

COLOR _____

ANIMAL (PLURAL) _____

ADJECTIVE _____

VERB _____

ADJECTIVE _____

PART OF THE BODY _____

NUMBER _____

CELEBRITY _____

VERB ENDING IN "ING" _____

VERB _____

NOUN _____

SILLY WORD _____

ADJECTIVE _____

ODE TO THE GREAT WHITE

The great white _____ rules the ocean—
NOUN

he's the king of the deep _____ sea.
COLOR

Schools of fish scatter like spooked _____
ANIMAL (PLURAL)

when they spot His Majesty.

This shark is a/an _____ hunter—
ADJECTIVE

he can _____ with exceptional speed.
VERB

He's known for a/an _____ sense of smell,
ADJECTIVE

and his _____ holds hundreds of teeth.
PART OF THE BODY

He has _____ more muscles than _____—
NUMBER   CELEBRITY

in short, this shark's a beast.

He's a lean, mean _____ machine that
VERB ENDING IN "ING"

lives to _____ and feast.
VERB

You don't ever want to come face-to-face

with this powerful _____-eating shark.
NOUN

Why not? _____! Because it's a fact
SILLY WORD

that his _____ bite is worse than his bark!
ADJECTIVE

MAD LIBS® is fun to play with friends, but you can also play it by yourself! To begin with, DO NOT look at the story on the page below. Fill in the blanks on this page with the words called for. Then, using the words you have selected, fill in the blank spaces in the story.

Now you've created your own hilarious MAD LIBS® game!

HOW TO MAKE A
SHARK TOOTH NECKLACE

VERB _____

ADJECTIVE _____

PART OF THE BODY (PLURAL) _____

A PLACE _____

ADJECTIVE _____

NOUN _____

NUMBER _____

ADJECTIVE _____

NOUN _____

PLURAL NOUN _____

NOUN _____

PART OF THE BODY _____

EXCLAMATION _____

PLURAL NOUN _____

PART OF THE BODY (PLURAL) _____

MAD LIBS®
HOW TO MAKE A
SHARK TOOTH NECKLACE

You don't need to _____ with sharks to show your love for
                       VERB

them. Try wearing a fashionably _____ shark tooth necklace
                                  ADJECTIVE

instead, made from fossilized _____ found in coastal
                               PART OF THE BODY (PLURAL)

areas around (the) _____. You can make one in a few steps:
                    A PLACE

1. Choose a/an _____ tooth, preferably a larger one,
                ADJECTIVE

   such as from a/an _____ shark.
                      NOUN

2. Tie approximately _____ inches of wire around each
                      NUMBER

   side of the _____ tooth and bring the ends together
                ADJECTIVE

   in the shape of a/an _____.
                         NOUN

3. Slide a cord made out of leather or _____ through
                                        PLURAL NOUN

   the loop. For extra flair, add a few _____-shaped
                                         NOUN

   beads along either side.

4. Tie the cord around your _____ and—
                             PART OF THE BODY

   _____!—you're done.
    EXCLAMATION

See? There's no need to spend a ton of _____ on this cool
                                        PLURAL NOUN

piece of jewelry when you can make one using your own two

_____.
PART OF THE BODY (PLURAL)

MAD LIBS® is fun to play with friends, but you can also play it by yourself! To begin with, DO NOT look at the story on the page below. Fill in the blanks on this page with the words called for. Then, using the words you have selected, fill in the blank spaces in the story.

Now you've created your own hilarious MAD LIBS® game!

SAFETY 101

VERB ENDING IN "ING" _____

NOUN _____

ADJECTIVE _____

VERB _____

TYPE OF LIQUID _____

ADJECTIVE _____

ADVERB _____

PLURAL NOUN _____

PART OF THE BODY _____

SILLY WORD _____

NOUN _____

COLOR _____

ANIMAL _____

NOUN _____

MAD LIBS®

SAFETY 101

How do you stay safe in the ocean where sharks could be

_____? Although encountering a/an _____
<u>VERB ENDING IN "ING"</u>   <u>NOUN</u>

while diving can be a thrilling experience, staying _____ is
                                                                      <u>ADJECTIVE</u>

your priority, and here are some ways to do that:

- First, scan the area where you want to _____.
                                                             <u>VERB</u>

  Enter the _____ quietly instead of making a/an
                  <u>TYPE OF LIQUID</u>

  _____ splash, so you don't surprise any sharks.
  <u>ADJECTIVE</u>

- Remain _____ alert and aware of your surroundings.
               <u>ADVERB</u>

- Stick close to the other _____ you are diving with.
                                       <u>PLURAL NOUN</u>

- Avoid making any sudden or erratic movements with your

  _____ or yelling "_____!" especially if
  <u>PART OF THE BODY</u>   <u>SILLY WORD</u>

  you spot a/an _____ fin circling the area.
                       <u>NOUN</u>

The great _____ shark, the bull shark, and the
                 <u>COLOR</u>

_____ shark are the most commonly encountered species.
<u>ANIMAL</u>

Always be respectful of them. Remember: You are invading their

_____, not the other way around!
<u>NOUN</u>

MAD LIBS® is fun to play with friends, but you can also play it by yourself! To begin with, DO NOT look at the story on the page below. Fill in the blanks on this page with the words called for. Then, using the words you have selected, fill in the blank spaces in the story.

Now you've created your own hilarious MAD LIBS® game!

WANTED: SHARK SCIENTIST

NUMBER _____

ADJECTIVE _____

VERB _____

TYPE OF LIQUID _____

SILLY WORD _____

PLURAL NOUN _____

A PLACE _____

VERB _____

VERB _____

ADJECTIVE _____

NOUN _____

VERB ENDING IN "ING" _____

ARTICLE OF CLOTHING (PLURAL) _____

NUMBER _____

PLURAL NOUN _____

NOUN _____

ADJECTIVE _____

VERB _____

MAD LIBS

WANTED: SHARK SCIENTIST

Do you love sharks? Could you spend _____ hours a day
NUMBER

studying one of the world's most fiercely _____ predators in
ADJECTIVE

their natural habitat? Are you fearless enough to _____
VERB

alongside them in _____ for research purposes? If you
TYPE OF LIQUID

answered "_____" to any of these questions, then we want
SILLY WORD

YOU to join our team of curious-minded _____ here at the
PLURAL NOUN

Oceanic Observatory in (the) _____ as we collect and
A PLACE

categorize all types of data on sharks—what they eat, where they

_____, how fast they _____, and more. While
VERB VERB

_____ experience is not required, priority consideration will
ADJECTIVE

be given to candidates who can expertly use sonar and other

_____ equipment. In addition, preference will be given to
NOUN

those skilled in swimming, scuba diving, and _____.
VERB ENDING IN "ING"

Wet suits and _____ for diving will be provided.
ARTICLE OF CLOTHING (PLURAL)

Starting salary is _____ _____ a month. Think
NUMBER PLURAL NOUN

you might be the right _____ for the _____ job of
NOUN ADJECTIVE

a shark scientist? Then _____ today for an application!
VERB

MAD LIBS® is fun to play with friends, but you can also play it by yourself! To begin with, DO NOT look at the story on the page below. Fill in the blanks on this page with the words called for. Then, using the words you have selected, fill in the blank spaces in the story.

Now you've created your own hilarious MAD LIBS® game!

A SHARK-INFESTED STORE

A PLACE _____

ADJECTIVE _____

NOUN _____

VERB _____

PART OF THE BODY (PLURAL) _____

ADJECTIVE _____

ARTICLE OF CLOTHING _____

NOUN _____

PART OF THE BODY _____

TYPE OF LIQUID _____

TYPE OF FOOD _____

NUMBER _____

ADJECTIVE _____

NUMBER _____

PLURAL NOUN _____

PERSON IN ROOM _____

CELEBRITY _____

VERB _____

MAD LIBS®

A SHARK-INFESTED STORE

When I was on vacation in (the) _____, I discovered
A PLACE

a/an _____ souvenir place near _____ Beach
ADJECTIVE NOUN

called the Shark Shop. This was a popular place where shark-loving

tourists like myself could come to _____. I couldn't believe
VERB

my _____ when I saw all the _____ shark
PART OF THE BODY (PLURAL) ADJECTIVE

stuff they stocked. I found a fun _____ that made you
ARTICLE OF CLOTHING

look like a hammerhead _____ when you put it on your
NOUN

_____. Next, I discovered a sporty water bottle that said
PART OF THE BODY

JAW-SOME! It was perfect for holding my _____.
TYPE OF LIQUID

My favorite find was _____-flavored shark gummies.
TYPE OF FOOD

I bought _____ pounds of those because they were so
NUMBER

deliciously _____! I gave the salesclerk _____
ADJECTIVE NUMBER

_____ to pay for my purchases. I couldn't wait to show my
PLURAL NOUN

cool new stuff to my shark-loving friends, _____ and
PERSON IN ROOM

_____. And I couldn't wait to come back to the Shark Shop
CELEBRITY

to _____ again soon!
VERB

MAD LIBS® is fun to play with friends, but you can also play it by yourself! To begin with, DO NOT look at the story on the page below. Fill in the blanks on this page with the words called for. Then, using the words you have selected, fill in the blank spaces in the story.

Now you've created your own hilarious MAD LIBS® game!

ADOPT A SHARK TODAY

PERSON IN ROOM _____

NUMBER _____

PLURAL NOUN _____

ADJECTIVE _____

CELEBRITY _____

NUMBER _____

NOUN _____

TYPE OF LIQUID _____

A PLACE _____

ANIMAL _____

ARTICLE OF CLOTHING _____

PART OF THE BODY _____

PLURAL NOUN _____

NOUN _____

A PLACE _____

NUMBER _____

ADVERB _____

PERSON IN ROOM _____

MAD LIBS®

ADOPT A SHARK TODAY

Dear _____:
   PERSON IN ROOM

Thank you for your generous donation of _____
                                            NUMBER

_____ to the Adopt-a-Shark program. Membership to our
PLURAL NOUN

program earns you these _____ benefits:
                          ADJECTIVE

- A framed Certificate of Adoption for "_____,"
                                          CELEBRITY

  a/an _____-pound _____ who lives in the
         NUMBER   NOUN

  _____ off the coast of (the) _____
  TYPE OF LIQUID   A PLACE

- A plush _____ and photo of your adopted pet
             ANIMAL

- A/An _____ to wear on your _____
         ARTICLE OF CLOTHING   PART OF THE BODY

- A tote bag to carry all your shark-themed _____
                                              PLURAL NOUN

- Free admission to any aquarium or other _____
                                            NOUN

  museum in (the) _____ and a/an _____
                   A PLACE   NUMBER

  percent discount on any merchandise in the gift shop

_____ yours,
ADVERB

_____, President
PERSON IN ROOM

MAD LIBS® is fun to play with friends, but you can also play it by yourself! To begin with, DO NOT look at the story on the page below. Fill in the blanks on this page with the words called for. Then, using the words you have selected, fill in the blank spaces in the story.

Now you've created your own hilarious MAD LIBS® game!

SHARK VS. DOLPHIN

PERSON IN ROOM _____

CELEBRITY _____

ADJECTIVE _____

PLURAL NOUN _____

ADJECTIVE _____

NOUN _____

EXCLAMATION _____

VERB _____

VERB _____

ADVERB _____

ADJECTIVE _____

TYPE OF LIQUID _____

PLURAL NOUN _____

VERB ENDING IN "ING" _____

NUMBER _____

PART OF THE BODY (PLURAL) _____

SHARK VS. DOLPHIN

This is Ace "Sharkface" McGinnis here with Dr. _____,
                                                PERSON IN ROOM
live from the shark vessel, the _____.
                                  CELEBRITY
Ace: Tell me, Doctor, which _____ creature would win in a
                                  ADJECTIVE
shark versus dolphin showdown?

Doctor: Most shark species have the advantage of size, power,

and _____. They are stealthy, _____ hunters, so
      PLURAL NOUN   ADJECTIVE
they can also sneak up on an unsuspecting _____ and—
                                            NOUN
_____!—it's game over! But that's not always enough.
 EXCLAMATION

Ace: It helps that dolphins can _____ faster than sharks, right?
                                      VERB
Doctor: Yes! Dolphins can usually out-_____ sharks
                                            VERB
in a chase. They are _____ intelligent and use a/an
                          ADVERB
_____ ability called echolocation to navigate through
 ADJECTIVE
_____ and communicate with their fellow _____
 TYPE OF LIQUID   PLURAL NOUN
in order to avoid sharks.

Ace: It's simple, though. Dolphins should stay away from where sharks

are _____ if they want to keep all _____ of
      VERB ENDING IN "ING"   NUMBER
their _____.
       PART OF THE BODY (PLURAL)

MAD LIBS® is fun to play with friends, but you can also play it by yourself! To begin with, DO NOT look at the story on the page below. Fill in the blanks on this page with the words called for. Then, using the words you have selected, fill in the blank spaces in the story.

Now you've created your own hilarious MAD LIBS® game!

SAVE THE SHARKS

NOUN _____

PLURAL NOUN _____

ADJECTIVE _____

ADJECTIVE _____

NOUN _____

A PLACE _____

VERB ENDING IN "ING" _____

TYPE OF LIQUID _____

PLURAL NOUN _____

ANIMAL (PLURAL) _____

A PLACE _____

VERB _____

ADJECTIVE _____

VERB ENDING IN "ING" _____

A PLACE _____

PLURAL NOUN _____

Sharks need our help! The Worldwide _____ Conservation
NOUN

Organization, which tracks whether _____ should be
PLURAL NOUN

classified as endangered, reports that an alarmingly high number of

shark species are close to becoming _____. Sharks are hunted
ADJECTIVE

for their _____ fins, which are used to make _____
ADJECTIVE NOUN

soup, considered a delicacy in many parts of (the) _____.
A PLACE

_____ in polluted _____ harms sharks, too.
VERB ENDING IN "ING" TYPE OF LIQUID

And sharks are often caught in netted _____ that are meant
PLURAL NOUN

to trap other _____. The increase in tourism in parts of
ANIMAL (PLURAL)

(the) _____ is yet another factor. Sharks use coastal areas to
A PLACE

feed, _____, and give birth to their _____ young,
VERB ADJECTIVE

but the development of vacation areas is wiping out this space for

sharks to use. Hunting, overfishing, and other _____
VERB ENDING IN "ING"

activities are badly affecting shark populations. If humans aren't

careful, sharks could disappear from (the) _____ very soon.
A PLACE

That wouldn't just be bad for the oceans, it would affect _____
PLURAL NOUN

everywhere!

Download Mad Libs today!

Join the millions of Mad Libs fans
creating wacky and wonderful
stories on our apps!